SHADOWCAT

POEMS

by

STERLING WARNER

ShadowCat: Poems
© 2008 Sterling Warner

This book may not be reproduced in whole or part, in any form (beyond that permitted by Sections 107 and 108 of the U.S. Copyright Law and except by reviewers for the purpose of criticism or review), without written permission the author

Printed in the United States of America.
Typeset by Rose Ingold
First Printing 2008

Maple Press
481 East San Carlos
San Jose, CA 95112
Phone: (408) 297-1000
Fax: (408) 297-1057
copy@maplepress.net
ISBN# 0-940-483-63-7

ShadowCat Poems

MOMENTS 1
    Grandma, the Flapper 2
    Snow 4
    TennisCoverage 6
    Raccoons and the British Invasion 8
    Sleepy Seattle 10
    Laissez Les Bons Temps Roule 12
    Continental Ballroom 14

BACKSTREETS 15
    Enigmas 16
    Celebrities 18
    The Warehouse 19
    Jesus Plays Guitar 20
    Myra Ellen 21
    Washington Depot 22
    Flirting with Mediocrity 24
    Graduate Students 25
    The Sequoias 26

NIGHTMARES 27

    Blues Hotel 28

    Mitigation: The Seizure 30

    Final Flight 36

    Survivor of Verdun 37

    Creature Feature 38

    Pleasure Point 39

    Swan Wings 40

AFTER THE SIGHS 41

    Mermaids 42

    You Too the Brown Earth Moves 44

    Mary Magdalene and I 46

    Faith 49

    Midsummer 50

    Encouragement 51

    Musings (You 52

    The Masseuse 54

    Memory (Hawaii 56

URCHINS ... 57

- Jigging It ... 58
- Exceptional Sights ... 60
- Big Apple Ad Lib ... 61
- White Coffin ... 62
- Haiku Sixte ... 63
- Haunting the Dead ... 64
- A Novice Caught Defacing Pictures ... 65
- The Cockpit ... 66
- Cosmic Commands ... 67

VIGNETTES ... 69

- Nets ... 70
- Stigmata ... 71
- Magnolia Massacre ... 72
- Preferences ... 73
- Holiday ... 74
- Smoking ... 74
- Tunnels ... 75
- Veins ... 75
- Pirate ... 76
- 2008: For Reginald Lockett ... 77

Sterling Warner

I
Moments

GRANDMA, THE FLAPPER

The Blackford girls
Roared with the 1920s; their
Short skirts scandalized—corrupted
Respectful Santa Clara County citizens;

Grandma fingered glass beads that
Hung around her neck like a rosary
As if lost in vespers, a new age soul, who
Rode the trolley downtown alone
Majored in Art at San Jose College
Imbibed alcoholic beverages and smoked, her
Tortoise shell cigarette holder long, unique;
Like Theda Bara, the Valley Vamp
Emancipated girlfriends previously
Bound by traditions,
School marm mentalities and
Social conventions.

An Egyptian diadem
Graced Grandma's brow
Wild Charleston arms fanned
Smoke filled speakeasies where
Prohibition possibilities
Created West Coast "wanna be"
Algonquin Roundtables;
All before stocks crashed, the
New Deal offered assurance, and
World War efforts began, she'd

Challenge gender inequity
Shatter glass ceilings, insist
Real heroes wore dresses—
Overalls while riveting.

Grandma, the flapper,
My Jazz Age heroine powdered
Her puritanical knees
Flaunted Blackford defiance; a
Spirit rebellious, ignoring decorum,
San Jose's original "it girl" became
Great-Grandfather's nightmare
Her hair bobbed,
Thick strand braided and
Placed to rest like a holy relic in
An antique cedar hope chest for
Remembrance—no regrets.

Grandma, who danced her legacy
"Backwards in heels," now
Rests undisturbed where all
Former flappers drink in private.

Snow

Smiles move across rooms
Like light rays glancing off mirrors
Heralding something special—the
Grandeur of moist breath on windshields
Morphing into geometric kaleidoscopes;
A white silence floating upon Northwest winds
Mt. Hamilton to Mt. Umunhum and beyond:
South Bay Area snow.

Road wet, highway
Slightly frozen
Snow Cats at the summit
Scrape black ice that
Spins cars face to face,
Slams multiple bumpers back to back
Slaps cautious drivers side to side, with airborne
Big rigs and compacts flying over embankments.

Indiscriminate, individual
Frenzied flakes fall
Briefly on Santa Cruz sand
Decorating the beach boardwalk,
Clinging to the Big Dipper among other
Amusement park rides with
Wafer-thin glacial blankets—
Layers of water frozen—resting, waning.

Seagulls pick frosty feathers,
Children rush onto the beach
Roll salty sand granules and kelp with
Melting winter wonderland flurries,
Creating slushy snowballs
Pelting each other as
Local telecasters film the rarity:
Weather, a lead story for the 11 p.m. news.

Tennis Coverage

Braided locks dance on
sunburned shoulders,
fiery wet skin pores, raging, rising
bouncing to tennis court rhythms,
drifting, shifting, bringing
blossoming bosoms into the night air.

Sooey!
preoccupied camera operators'
carpal tunnel thoughts,
swing to new levels of alertness
with signature grunts and pig calls,
echoing cross-court;
high velocity, canned adrenaline explodes,
graphite rackets press balls forward.

"What a shot! Right down the line,"
notes a commentator
while camera lenses wander to
nipples hard and stiff—close up shots
everyone pretends not to notice—
though teenage boys and middle-aged men
secretly imagine the aureoles
beneath each damp sports bra.

When players get down to familiar postures
cameras zoom in on tight asses—
the Grafs, Kornakovas, Mauresmos,
Navratilovas, Sabatinis, Seles,
Sharopovas, Williams sisters, Ivanovics . . .
tennis queens past and present—
as if to capture important archival footage of
      "good taste,"
twisted like bicycle spokes,
      hip to hub.

RACCOONS & THE BRITISH INVASION

Raccoons plagued
Uncle Glenn's corn patch one summer
cracking sweet corn ears,
sleeping in arms of any
scarecrow standing sentry,
several weeks before my uncle
centered radios in the field,
facing four directions
blasting Mantovani into pitch black,
overriding night's songs,
a cricket chorus. The raccoons' eyes glowed
like dance floor lights as they dipped, swayed, and
sashayed in their eternal hand washing

The British invasion marched upon Uncle Glenn—
Music he despised—when
we descended on his farm for the summer.
Nature's bandits, raccoons,
recognized the charge
never again washing hands to muzak
driving surf rhythms,
maudlin teenage death songs, or
James Brown's soul music—

Cousins'd gather annually at the farm,
bunking in a shack
kitty-corner to the patch;
dusk 'til dawn; dawn 'til dusk, we'd
argue 'bout whose hair's longest, as
Mick Jagger belted "Satisfaction"
through the darkness and we religiously listened,
having no complaints, yet the
raccoons loathed the Union Jack minstrels;
Richards' guitar licks, Jagger's voice
sent them running like ground squirrels
pursued by wild fires, as we
gestated in our rock 'n roll dream womb—
at least 'til that summer's end—
not to return, fanciful teens
becoming less and less like our
free spirited, music liberators than
raccoons pursued by British tunes.

SLEEPY SEATTLE

for Bill Swanson

Seattle simmers, sunlight wanes
Tripping up and down the
Space needle like a
Slide trombone on end
Moving along, evening hours
In the groove, reminding
All *aficionados* the city's Grunge and
Lesbian punk eclipsed any tune
Crafted and cut by the Village People

Night crawling eyes
Cut through rot-gut bourbon,
Inch across each smoky dive;
Bloodshot orbs rest,
Recover, hide behind
Dark heroin shades or
Rose tinted glasses,
Observe the jam; bodies
Nod, listen, channel;

Midnight shadows 'til intrusive dawn light
Blowing changes, mixing the coda
Hastens the "jazz funk" fusion,
Develops genuine timbre out of
Sloppy touches, negotiates turnarounds
Note building upon note,
Plucking occasional bluesy riffs
Side stepping mainstream,
Hanging on the Improv cymbal;

Bill, once disco overshadowed rock
Neutralizing authenticity, leeching the
Vitality of a genuine musical *Chi*,
Jazz gushed through your veins
Like fast flowing streams down
Mount Rainier—phat, cool,
Unpredictable—moving into double time,
Call and response, flatted fifths,
Bebop, and piano chord voicings.

LAISSEZ LES BONS TEMPS ROULE

For Hurricane Katrina's Victims

Katrina's torrent barely touched Vieux Carré.
It endures on high ground where the
Café Du Monte stands like a citadel,
Issues dark roasted Chicory Coffee 24/7,
Dusts powdered sugar on Beignet loving patrons;
No swampland crypt, the French Quarter presents
Pedestrians with a sanctuary to suck down *safe* hurricanes
Chased with "Harry's Huge Beers."

Voodoo lovers slap legs together
Like alligator tails in brackish marshes;
Balcony flirts, evening ladies wear delicate masks
Fat Tuesday, last day before Lent's forty-day fast;
Mardi Gras magic exudes from every pore,
Elaborately costumed krewes toss beads off floats,
Give rise to fanciful celebrations of the dead,
Historic carnival steeped in Catholic doctrine.

Haitian halos encircle heads,
Bend minds, create
Sober motley moments among
Tarot card readings, psychic oracles
Jostling Bourbon Street crowds—
Backdrop for parading ramblers,
Mischievous, Puckish vagabonds,
Ragged marching saints.

Shuffling along as
Jazz bands blow Dixieland
Zydeco singers scrape wash boards, and
Street musicians mutter the blues,
Encouraged by two hands clapping,
Living dreams off guitar case offerings:
Copper tokens, silver coins,
Green paper gratitude.

Gris, Gris in my pocket, still
Scaling steps in New Orleans
Looking down Toulouse Street
Finding JAX Brewery gone
Replaced by Planet Hollywood. No
Mississippi miracle could heal Katrina survivors
Cleanse the river, recover such culture—
Foreboding yet enticing Gothic glamour.

The Continental Ballroom

for Jim Morrison

"The End" notched our souls
with beginnings,
lying in the shadows of
the Lizard King's mantra
pressing bodies on the
Continental Ballroom floor
smoking joints,
drinking peppermint schnapps,
sharing cigarettes,
stepping into bathrooms,
highs lost in porcelain exaltations,
reciting philosophies about
war, peace, hate, love,
imagining ourselves
back door men or
free spirited women
confronting the status quo,
meditating on a lyric
dazed, numb, radiant in tune with
a backdrop of liquid
kaleidoscope lightshows,
oils separating, reforming,
like rainbow amoebas—
ultimate shape shifters
assuming no definite form—
credentials worthy of Morrison's
Dionysian fellowship.

II
BACKSTREETS

Enigmas

Like an ice palace during
A free skate,
Everyone's on edge
Chipping away
While rappers twizzle
Laying out on the gold chains
Pontificating values of the hood,
Showcasing precious metals

So when's the last time you been back to
Sleepless streets, alleys that never yawn,
Strategic thoroughfares that initiate
Nike photo-op footwork?
Pacing forms pop jump after jump
Create slinky shadows behind
Warped plywood plank backboards
Braided wire hanger hoops where
Rim shots morph each fragile circle until
Nothing drops through—
Only imaginations slam, dunk, spin in
Another universe without traveling.

Remember Friday afternoons?
High school kids choking on silver whistles
Bullies tossing tied tennis shoes over
Low hanging power lines, sometimes
Walking home barefoot, victimized by
A familiar hustle, their own hostile game?
Escape artists, misty eyed dreamers
Like Sufis, shamen, fakirs, and aesthetics
Center their social paralysis and
Disenchantment, find solace in
Future tattoos, exotic piercings
Becoming thoughtful enigmas,
Legends in their own minds.

CELEBRITIES

Hey John John
Princess Diana
we grieved your passing, but
the world's not at an end; it
just lost more innocence,
hope, possibilities
championed through causes,
projected by people.
the media had it wrong.
Nothing stopped at all; television
specials went into production the
second someone thought
there would be a chance
of gore, death, mayhem, misfortune
possibilities of boosting ratings.

Indignant, self-righteous,
we scorned media excesses while
spurring them onward,
viewing what we could,
whenever,
making coverage competitive, a
broadcasting bonanza,
catapulting yet another
social nightmare into
prime time entertainment.

So it went with 9/11, when
Infotainment shifted gears,
fear and alarm ruled the day
featured looped footage
showcasing *Air Jets* on impact to
toppling twin towers; astonished,
stunned by the random act of
terrorism, lectured time and again,
"our lives changed forever the day" a
highjacker handful reminded
world citizens of United States vulnerability.

THE WAREHOUSE

Sawdust rain buckets everywhere
feed and grain sacks stacked high
on scarred, splintered floors
cold, damp, noisy
rain glances off the metal roof like
arrows pelting Achilles' shield.

Gutted warehouse, hollow anvil
a tin can shell supported by beams bowing
old, enduring, merciless,
especially in the summer months,
when the sun's rays beat upon silver walls, and
workers feel enclosed inside a deep skillet.

JESUS PLAYS GUITAR

Jesus plays guitar
Weeping like Lorca,
At the Catalyst,
Sustains diminished chords
Picks tasty licks celebrating
Humanity, spirituality, love,
Resonating silent compassion
Through hands pierced & bloody
Instead of
Hanging over altars
Advertising life, death, resurrection—
Secret mysteries—
Befitting Bacchus, Bromius
Dionysus or Osiris.

Jesus strums above the doorway
Notes filtering
Over heads every color
Bodies pierced in
Every orifice & then some . . .
He nods towards inheritors of
All that's dynamic & meek,
Troubadours of the future,
Singing "carpe diem"
To the tune of
Good deeds &
Eternal testimonies.

MYRA ELLEN

Heads as individual as red cabbage
Roll to music, pulsating, piercing
Maroon shades run into black jets, people in
Lace mourning dresses,
High fashion glitter,
Designer slacks, and
Denim overalls
Ears and feet at mass receive
High communion, a host of
Identity, spirituality, restoration;
Facing the smoke machine altar with
Inanna at the keyboards
Bemused by fairy-winged fans who start moving
As she strikes each new tune
Some writhing from "Spark" to "Hey Jupiter,"
"Blood Roses" to "Cornflake Girl,"
Sitting, standing, dancing, sitting,
Sitting, standing, dancing, sitting,
Sitting, standing, dancing, sitting;
Others straining above, below, and beside the
Gyrating forms for a
Glance of their icon.

WASHINGTON DEPOT

Shaved heads, rainbow hair grace
Bodies glorifying eclectic fashion.
Pressing into complete strangers,
Classic, sculptured breasts
Proudly pronounce
"This is why I'm hot" behind
T-shirts stretched like nylons
Over vibrant torsos.

Indifferent voices speak on cell phones,
Hotlines to Homeland Security,
Wait like pacing wildcats in
A bus line that coils its way
Through the track dog terminal,
Snakes out into a street
Hostile to everyone, everything,
From sunshine to gutter spit.

Senior citizens and children
Board the Greyhound bus
Sit shoulder to shoulder,
Every seat taken, breathe
Recycled oxygen, gasp the
Unwholesome atmosphere, exhale like a
Forced air furnace sputtering in a corner
Where not even parasites can survive.

The fox-fur woman's thighs balloon,
A shaky gelatin mass, as her
Butt spreads like a squashed slug,
Cellulite inching under my armrest;
She pushes her body next to mine
Demands the driver switch off
Cool air circulating among sweaty
Passengers. He obliges; we wallow

Silver hair cascades on ample breasts of a
Birkenstock junkie, a leather-faced woman
Who's worked on far too many tans; she
Suns herself where one shin meets a foot,
Showcases a spider web tattoo,
Black widow ready to pounce.
Clinging, encircling her ankle,
Dropping to her toes.

White shirt mannequin—
Polyester suit enthusiast—a
Backseat evangelist unfastens
A duct-taped carry-on, then
Sanctimoniously passes out
Little green Bibles to
New commuter passengers as if
Dealing them blessed hands of poker.

Bus riders avoid "the word"
Like a jury summons, reverentially stuffing
Minute plastic covered missives in
Magazine pockets behind each seat
Swaying in unison like a choir,
Each time the vehicle lurches left, shifts right
—So distinctive, so typical, bus culture
Rolling from Seattle, Tacoma, Olympia

FLIRTING WITH MEDIOCRITY

Flirting with mediocrity
vulture eyes that winked once too often
feathered red lines extend across the whites
crows-feet sprout in the corners
egalitarian grandeur
against *mass* Munchkin preciousness
a ballooning *suck-up* body
bursts buttons on
handmade Italian
pin-striped suits.

Limp wristed, collapsed fingers
shake other hands—a half-hearted ritual,
more self-conscious networking
than mutual salutation . . .
distant, far from close scrutiny,
immune to harsh judgment, criticism, and insults
working towards a personal illusion:
better at intimidation, cosmetic appearances—
lust breathing life into mediocrity.
Pressing others to disregard genuine standards,
Skippy, the wanna-be Zeus,
like an outgoing sentry,
pats backs, feigns laughter,
mutters, "Here's my new paradigm,"
frequently distracted by
statuesque legs, bare knees,
sheer stockings, or fishnet hose.

GRADUATE STUDENTS

We were all too serious once
writing undaunted phrases in abstract perfection
unaware of sophisticated cliché, or
        verse like lumpy gravy
precocious, passionate and purposeful,
summoning the muse,
expecting inspiration
        so sure of the uncertain world's design.

Sidney, we knew your *Apologie for Poetrie*
took to heart each syllable of *A Well Wrought Urn;*
where to now vague memory, vagrant guide—
        slothful creater of knowledge?
Back to *Poetics* or forward to *Frye* ?
Will earnest overcome mediocrity, or
continue to perpetuate dissatisfaction?
        Once, we thought, our viewpoints matured.

THE SEQUOIAS

For Phil Persky

Wings clipped, losing plumage,
Snowy Egrets slowly shuffle and roll into
Dining commons or elevator gateways to
Private rooms with panoramic views;
Hunched, visages downcast,
Faintly lit eyes cautiously
Inspect carpeted, linoleum, hardwood floors
Before each two, three, six-legged step.

Many spotted like leopards, they
Wait for something secret, someone special to
Lift them from twilight,
Bring on rainbow radiance:
A movie, card game, nostalgic song,
Soap opera, any thrill—anticipating
Visitors who left their sides
Only two minutes earlier, a lifetime ago.

Confusing the living and deceased,
Confiding in familiar strangers more often than
Friends and family whose faces mirror names
Dropped from shriveled lips—some
Carelessly adorned in scarlet paint—residents linger
Puzzled, bewildered, uncertain who
They'll be grieving, honoring, missing at
The Sequoias' next memorial.

III
NIGHTMARES

BLUES HOTEL

Two Jacksons or
Four sawbucks
Up front—$40.
No credit cards, no I.D.;
Beyond, beneath,
Battered neon lights
The Blues Hotel
Weathered time's ravages
Struck chords of commerce as
Hookers dispense advice
Like ATM machines—
Service for a price.

Soiled linen, wafer thin sheets, feel and
Look like pillow drool on flax
A ceramic throne, standard toilet,
Sits on splintered two-by-fours,
Wax ring smashing like a plum
Slightly sinking like a rock in thick mud when
seated.
Yellow halos ripple over textured ridges,
Plaster summits, on the
Sparkling stucco ceiling where
Snow seeps through the roof
Dripping tears into a closet
That seldom houses luggage.

Here on Colfax, cops draw down on
Wendy's customers—mistake naive
Travelers as "King's Table" players—
Denver's whorehouse clientele,
Crack den magistrates.
One's next-door neighbors'
Fists pound paper-thin walls like
Meat tenderizers pummeling flesh or
Jack hammers cracking concrete;
Rattling door handles twist, turn
Voices chant incantations, grunt outside
Demand immediate admittance—
Ready to fix a need, a place to
Tie down before daylight resumes
Kickin' flop house reality,
The Blues Hotel's legacy, above,
Below, and on all sides of every room.

MITIGATION: THE SEIZURE

I

Quivering limbs, a plain of torn lips,
Neural spasms—writhing, clenching;
Like Proteus I change face and form,
But this liquid masque is not of my choosing;
    it conforms to no occasion.
Naked power spirits it onward
To a soul, no less than mortal measure,
    seeking sanctuary,
Release from an abyss of immortality—
              the facade—
That sphere of indifference, realm of uncertainty.

Pale Hecate, your bitchy, bewitching ways
Contort and twist my frame incessantly.
    (This is damnation, no holy sickness)
Preserve your barbed gift devoid of symmetry;
    wave your torch at a distance . . . .
Never was I dipped in the River Styx,
My hide is all heel, sinew, mucus, and blood;
So why spare me the deluge I cannot ever see?
Let me flow with its tide and cease this malaise,
Wherein cognizance only follows its doleful devastation,
Surviving to experience its rabid force
    again.
To live as Prometheus, and see life through
    a shadow,
Each day to remember and cringe—once again.

II

Ecstatic moments before the flood
Darkness encroaches— (I grow frightened).
One prison to another, my journey's begun
From the chains of self-reproach
To the bonds of old oblivion,
        I limp helplessly forward
Clinging tightly to Morpheus with heavy hopes
        (Make it different this time, make it different).
But in that ebon dungeon of unrest,
Where I am Hephaestus and
        my cell is Olympus,
There I see all smiles as contrived,
I hear the sound of laughing children as cries of woe,
Find the smell of fresh-cut flowers offensive.
My deformed feet solely limp backwards;
I cannot correct my bent, crooked posture,
Or peer over emaciated faces
        with rose bud cheeks . . . .
Horrible beauty, perplexing apparition,
We're too familiar with one another
        (You must change, I must change, we both must change!)

        the flood is over . . . .

Life I've known you only through shadows,
Through shadows I cringe at you
        once again.

Wrath of Achilles abates in my anatomy,
Awaking to a sordid stillness, a hush
An audience agrees, nodding heads
        this performance was worse than the last one.
But they will applaud, and
They will pretend; in kindness they'll say
        "Nothing went wrong . . .
                please sleep.
Sleep, sleep, sleep; now you must sleep.
You've just had a fall and need to sleep."
"No!" I insist, face full of fury,
Lashing out to avenge bloody Patroclus;
(But am I not loathed Hector too?)
For a moment, perhaps, I will lie down,
In that time an answer might be found
        still nothing.

Why must merciful faces become hovering Harpies
Once my journey has come full circle?
What comfort can I glean from their intentions?
        (I will not sleep—not now)
My throat yet moist with drops from the Lethe
Does little to enhance recollection
        (How did I look? What did I do?)
Why won't they tell me what I don't remember?
        that which I have never witnessed?
                (In time, perhaps, in due time)
Eyes just bathe my body with sympathy,

They've seen naught but a miserable exterior:
> a frenzied shroud, a stranger to me.
>> Is there no more to this than a fall?
> my harrowing of hell, my whimpering retreat?

Should I tell them of my darker malady?
That I've been far beyond the confines of this floor—
> to chambers where promise is a past time,
>> where crying's sinister. praise contempt?
Am I absurd to ignore their advice and concern?
> They've seen me here many times before;
> I've seen them weeping above me before.

III

Good physician, Apollo, heal me
For cavernous wounds abide unattended,
Ragged tissue adorns my temples,
Scars inside my head are many.
Pull your radiance across my sky;
Dispel those shadows lurking below.
My Dionysian discomfort may soon relapse
As the Maenads attack and sever my parts,
Casting them to deserts unknown to humans,
> forgotten by the immortals.
(I fear the time my dismembered limbs
> *will not be found and reunited,)*
Phoebus Apollo, guide me with light,
Son of Leto, gift me with control . . . .

> *. . . Must I heal myself?*

What life can coral blood sustain

In a parched inferno ribbed with ashen stones?
Through the whipping wave of heat
      my marrow is scattered,
          crushed into fine powder,
     while I froth and utter
         revolting sounds.
But I am surely not a martyr, a sacrificial life;
Each stone was put into place by myself.
Nonetheless, a knife remains above me, and
I am champion, priest, and altar for my cause;
         nothing's less fair!
For how can I--ever--raise my guard
To deflect the stroke of an affliction
Whose brazen strength resides unshackled,
      omnipotent and unseen?

Yet if I should bow to affliction's design,
Days of torment, weeks lying fallow,
Would I be any more than the lamb or the goat
      repeating an equivocal ritual?
Or would I merely exist as a splintered talon,
     grasping for beauty, searching for perfection?
I am not Ganymede, nor is Ganymede me;
My spirit's eternalized by difference—not demand.
        (An eternity has had its price)
My own cup's spilt full of dissatisfaction;
Beauty cloaks the crisis of crossed identity
For two equal one, yet the total is three

IV

All apples of Eris thrown in my midst
Are nothing more than vintaged cider;
The decision, hereof, will not lead to Troy.
I've already breached the walls of Ilium, and
Have seen the confusion—scared worried faces—
      wet trembling hands and fearful sad eyes;
I knew their grim countenance too well.
There's no reason to create havoc anew;
      I've no time to resume that battle—
          nor have they the strength to fight it.

Sporadic confrontation with yon Breathing Quietus,
Where true identity is subjectively perceived,
      we shall not sojourn so often.
Though the Sirens beckon, urge prompt visitation,
Their song does not attract me.
Yes, their convocation will only cause them frustration,
For the parts I've played for Melpomene
      shall be no more;
          lack of rehearsal has made me weary.
I will pluck the strings on Orpheus' lyre,
    Move aged Hades to tears
    (I won't glance back at myself—I won't glance back)
    Even though the Moerae sharpen sheers and wait,
    Holding the threads linking two in one body
    I won't glance back
    Sisyphus and I are at rest . . . .

FINAL FLIGHT

Green golf course turf flickers on TV,
Velvet throat announcer softly speaks as
If recanting secret rites
Only life-like sound/sight upon entering
Grandma's bedroom.
Kool nonfilters, bent like charred straws—
One end, a scarlet blot, the other a black coal—
Jammed into an ashtray overflowing,
Mahogany bedside, zebra striped,
Glass of Lord Calvert, color of weak tea,
Adding moisture rings to the
Scarred legacy of cigarette butts,
Suggested something then I noticed
Silk ash remnants of her billowing peignoir,
Bedroom through kitchen,
Kitchen through dining room,
Dining room into hallway, a
Trail of final moments led to the
Main bathroom where grandma
Concluded her flight,
Third degree burns covering her
Gentle body, screaming skin now at peace,
Lodged in a corner . . . .
Pupils wide, countenance bewildered,
Her terrorized, tortured state,
Pain immeasurable, still haunts me, and I
Wonder why I hesitated
Closing eyes I'd never
Look into again, and questioned the coroner's
Conclusion, "She passed on due to a heart attack."

SURVIVOR OF VERDUN

Father loved you for food scraps
tossed his way after
cleaning your house while in college.
Then, you graced my parent's marriage with
a moth eaten copy of your book,
A Survivor of Verdun (a lie),
dedicated solely to the groom.

From benedictions to revivals,
mantras to mosques,
changing religions
more often than your clothes, you
always felt superior,
claiming fellowship with Einstein and
men of vision, living in a world
without women, respect for yourself—
an insignificant man with
no right to anyone's memory.

Yet I recall you
intruding uninvited at
mother's doorstep—edges of
my nightmares, a demon speaking tongues—
ghastly, calloused, hideous, and vain—
forbidden incubus, clouding,
confusing father with
tales of torment and affliction,
human dramas that taught you the
arrogance of a martyr
tossing stones at himself,
delighting in the attention
never allotted to others, all of us
commoners, unworthy inhalers of
fresh air made polluted each time you breathed.

CREATURE FEATURE

Like a blue energy cluster, coalescing into an
Intricate maze of switches, steel rings, gigantic gauges—
High voltage dials, current conductors,
Electrodes feed lightning bolt's children
Flickering sparks, hot current, to
Dysfunctio Cerebri, an Abnormal Brain.
"It's alive! It's alive!" Colin Clive
Cries as eyes roll, muscles twitch: The modern
Prometheus, Baron Von Frankenstein's
Creature, walks among us.

Lon Chaney Jr. resurrected yet again
Scratches a pentagram scar, recollects,
Listens for creaky wagons, seeks
Gypsy guidance, spiritual fortitude,
Hangs on each mad scientist's promise of a lycanthropic cure
Buys a new pair of shoes after each full moon
Dramatically shape shifts in convenient mirrors
Twitches his jowls after mascara darkens features and
Documents his hair growth with a time lapse camera
Escapes to the wild woods, hip deep in dry ice.

The Man of a Thousand Faces—Béla, Boris, Elsa, Vincent,
Vampira—household names, best loved films from the
Phantom of the Opera to *The House of Dracula*,
The Bride of Frankenstein to *The Mummy Returns*,
Universal Studios thrived filming thrilling horror movies;
Rake-brandishing villagers, sewer-marching citizens
Brought an end to evil in each black and white flick
Paved the way for new beginnings: Lizard-like aliens
Psychotic taxidermists, reluctant exorcists,
Teenage werewolves, scores of the living dead.

Pleasure Point

Greenback tides reaching, arcing
imploding sand where
poetry of motion exalts dynamic
power, beauty, voice
as tidal tiers of salty arms—the
ocean's altars—enclose, embrace, uproot.

We were there.
Red kelp stretching across the bay
floating like linked rubies,
priceless, alluring;
between a horseshoe rock cluster
we scrambled down, drew marks
set sand slicing records
hurried back up the smug boulder cradle;
I drew the line none dared duplicate.

Brief traveling moments from sand cove to safety,
half way up, a wave cracked my back, sent me sliding
into a toilet bowl of sandblasting surf;
struggling, swimming, numb, senseless,
endorphins kicked in,
neutralizing sensations of body piercing buckshot—
sand grains and sharp coral pumped into arms, legs, and torso.
No bright lights, divine voices singing—just 14 years flashing,
chestnut arms flailing, protesting the sea's determined
undertow, like an irrepressible tsunami,
dragging across the sea.

As the wave receded, I clutched onto crab crags
at the bottom of the horseshoe,
instinctively climbing to higher ground, yet
over my shoulder, still another wave appeared,
curled over my head, as I slipped down the mossy rock back.

Thoughts of drowning washed across my mind
retreated like waves ebbing, sands shifting,
picturing my mother's face collapsing like wet paper,
the news cutting, wounding her
like the coral scraping my back—yet nothing but
mad spinning and lungs burning for air kept me going.

Slammed into the cove's hub
water pummeled me like a butter churn dasher,
pushing my hamburger body upwards
where I caught hold of a hand.

IV
AFTER THE SIGHS

Mermaids

"I know you want to get rid of your fish's tail, and to have two supports instead of it, like human beings . . . . Put out your little tongue that I may cut it off as my payment."

—*The Little Mermaid*, The Brothers Grimm

Iridescent sea foam crests like fireflies flickering on
Warm summer evenings, orchestrates night sounds,
Touches inner pulsations. Waiting, watching, pressing hands
We gaze beyond tamarisk waves lapping sandy beaches:
Enchantment's doorway—where
People, places, things remain ever-present.

Perched upon rugged rocks that break the glass faced ocean
Mermaids take coral combs, groom exquisite hair—
Amber, charcoal, golden, red, silver, sepia—luxurious locks,
Concealing bare breasts and slim stomachs;
Emerald fish tails flashing, slapping volcanic thrones and aquatic mists,
Consciously flirting with the world above and deep waters below.

Sweet Siren voices beckon as separate sea songs merge:
Gulls cry, whales talk back and forth—accentuating
Silent moments with majestic sonar blasts—while
Dolphins chatter, waves crash, and inanimate life forms chime in:
Foghorns bellow like long *rag-dung* Tibetan trumpets,
Buoyed bells clang, little lights glimmer through fog.

Reclining on peaking waves, salt water pillows,
Lounging atop skeletal ships—mariner graveyards,
Relaxing on sultry barnacle barstools,
Mermaids serenade sea creatures and sailors—anything adrift;
Seaweed laurels crown innocence, cloak mischievous minds in
Curiosity's veil; they belong to no *person*—no *thing*

Alluring, compelling, disturbing: the inquisitive caretakers swim into
Mysterious sea caverns, sunken galleon treasures, subconscious
Depths where humans imagine themselves feral sea children,
Watery soul mates never required to choose between fins or legs—
Graceful tails or knife piercing footsteps—life and death whirlpools,
Sea witches' propositions and unquestioned sacrifice.

You Too the Brown Earth Moves

for Alma

Alma, you too the
brown earth moves
Gaea's song, your mantra
your hand—a compass
your heat—all humanity
your sweat—renewal.

Mixing rhythmic movements with
terrace winds
facing barstool acclaim,
disdaining dance eugenics
feet moving,
back arching,
legs spinning.

You were there when strobe lights
glanced off a revolving
multi-mirrored ball,
shot fireflies across the room,
wooden
dance floor empty,
enticing, yet intimidating to a
younger crowd *clubbing it*
people who just witnessed
peers engaged in
precision drills—
Motown madness—
synchronized motion . . . .

They saw you float freely
felt the music—
sensed your gypsy soul—
watched you
at ease,
wanted your
instruction, your steps,
approval of borrowed gestures,
mastery over twirls—
knowledge of
inner rainbows.

You responded up-tempo,
arms beckoning, smile assuring,
spilling confidence indiscriminately—
powerfully—like
rain cascading over gutters
anointing, initiating hesitant bodies
into a dance they might have missed.

MARY MAGDALENE AND I

Before the *J. C. Superstar* cast convenes
Exotic Mary sensuously glides
Customer to customer like a lap-dancer
Her petite breasts as round
As delicacy permits
So, so close—never making contact
Artiste's dharma true to the
Magdalene shuffle, no
Footstep feels devotion's pebble; no
Commitment compromises advantage as
She stirs hearts across the stage,
Teaches me songs of love unrequited
Says that teardrops shed *grace* that all
People endure, as well anointed shrines of
Pain, purpose, kindness, elegance,
Passion against their enemies
Leaves audiences wanting even more.

Receptive spirit, Mary's *chutzpah*
Like a summer shower all but baptizes
Parched spiritual wastelands,
Revives faith, fulfills empty promises,
Gifts troubled troubadours
With a gesture, a thought;
Hair ebony, eyes ultraviolet, her
Femme fatale tongue licks the air
Like a blessed monarch
Butterfly—mouth uncurling,
Vermillion lips spreading,
As if collecting youth preserving
Nectar, yes, ambrosia for some
Fair weather Messiah (or me).

Almost a date, a few momentary
Thoughts embracing your figure through
Winchester *Bay View* Bakery's window
Simple glances that prance around customers
Like fairy feet barely kissing enchanted
Forest floors gazed over my shoulder—
Far beyond the glass; there the
Female apostle with an approximate smile,
Invites inquisitions, discourages hesitations
Sets the world at sixes and sevens
Nearly offering tenderness—practically touching
Me with hands like crushed velvet
Consummating our casement relationship.

Like an experienced *doula*,
Soaking up midnight's essence, Mary
Kept company with pale, tetchy apparitions,
Lost souls searching, circling,
Meandering over serrated
Imaginations, fluted daydreams,
Edgy night time visions; there
Her shape-shifting gospel spreads like
Shade beneath an eagle's wingspan,
Protective shadow hanging over my head,
Plummeting into a heart shackled,
Bruised by confusion's restraints,
Desire's dimmer purposes.

With measured muted conversation
Brassy laughter lines highlighting smiles
Practically speak to me, conveying
Lipstick messages; then
Our eyes finally lock and
Like Ouija Boards guiding
Fingertips atop flat planes divining
Information from disembodied spirits,
We scan each other, affirm suspicions,
Paint ourselves with restriction's brushstrokes
Frame our visual courtship—
An almost approachable
Windowpane romance—
Knowing neither how to cultivate nor
Nurture an *Affaire de Coeur,*
Advance imagination any further. So
Forget the performance,
Leave one of seven veils behind
A trivial, poignant reminder,
We never knew how to love.

FAITH

Eyes like faded gaslights
Dim; arms ache, bones
Abrasive like frictional matches that
Ignite arthritic infernos, fuel
Carpal tunnel retribution;
Such moments found
Faith an attractive alternative to
Life's snowdrift melting into
Nothingness, death.

Faith endured like a gospel choir,
Intoning words of praise rising above
Life celebrated, mortality honored
A stately chorale wherever she walked, her
Words rigidly whispered solidarity's song,
Mint tea fresh and Lolita-like, Faith
Lip-locked all youthful rites of passage
As if hers were the first.

Midsummer

She took both my hands
held them breast high, then
gazed at me like a prized photograph
undressed me with her eyes
bathed me in her tears
blessed me with soft sighs
reassured me with spontaneous smiles—
        dream moments as healing
        as the Pool of Bethesda, or
        Ponce de León's fountain.

Return in full costume
learn your lines well that
we may speak through character
moving with the cadence
breaking the fourth wall as
star-crossed lovers, medieval misfits,
or renaissance courtiers
        black sail on the horizon . . . yet
        perfectly matched somewhere along
        slumber's crossroads.

Let me back into the dream
where buttons pronounce readiness
malapropisms drop like
frogs from the sky
you anoint me with travesties
irreversible laughter
unadulterated touches
consummated whispers
        trust impish shadows, as
        comforting as a feather bed, that
        honor all mischievous illusions.

ENCOURAGEMENT

"You seem different."
Three simple words
echoed in my head as she
kissed my cheek with
lips like finely painted
porcelain China: red,
cool, soft, full, fragile—bloodless—
sufficient means of transport into
livery stable romantic bliss;
there our knotted energy exploded
like a candy-filled piñata into
passion's nightlights;
wafer-thin steel blades,
silver against the onyx sky,
glanced off your hair as if parried by
a shield, absorbing, testing,
spinning straw tresses into
blonde slivers, golden threads.

MUSINGS (YOU)

You, my better poem
One I didn't create, I
Could read your lines
Daily, a lifetime,
With full satisfaction,
New appreciation
You
Majesty's Metaphor
Jeweled fingers curled
Around a crystal stem,
I that
Wine glass leg, patiently stand,
Top to bottom, palm oil anointed
Breathing hands exalt
Celestial prisms, spreading
Inward
You the blue, I the red in
Violet eyes where I
Fragmented verse, Imperfection's symbol,
Lie in wait, a misguided pulsar

Like an acceptable
Percentage of insect
Body parts within
Bulk food bins,
Undetectable, yearning
To be touched, acknowledged,
Received as the holiest of communions

You,
A perfect sestina,
You were supposed to
Personify youth
Eternally
Sanctifying a memory—
That singular beach boardwalk
Photograph
Hanging above my bed
Like a crucifix—rather than
Caged mortality, my
Unfinished couplet

The Masseuse

Face sticking through a padded white doughnut
Closed eyes envision azure skies,
Vermillion clouds, a comforting response to
Unfamiliar, all too welcome caresses of
A skilled expressive artisan whose
Hands stroke every muscle imaginable
Releasing tension, encouraging exaltation—
Words, sounds—oohhs and ahhs uttered
Only in moments intimate.

Kneading, reshaping my back, body, thighs with
All the subtlety of inner-city sidewalks
Pressing against footsteps—casting
Singular appreciation,
Undivided attention
The deep tissue *masseuse* moves her
Fluid fingers over a body tired
Activating metabolic mysteries—an
Orgasmic ritual initiation into reflexology.

Electrifying limbs, stimulating senses
From aromatherapy to
Crackling chiropractics while mood music
Filters through quadraphonic speakers
Bounces off each dimly lit wall—
Thin blankets of dusk—
Sails to the ceiling, lingers, then
Drops like a thin threadless canopy, toe to head
Becomes serenity's uniform cloak.

Exiting Optimum Health Management
Feeling like a sculptor's finest achievement
I emerge as the masseuse's masterpiece
Each muscle at ease, every joint relaxed,
Thirty-three vertebrae aligned,
Sensual not sexual, body harmony
Magical massage moments,
Like a severely addictive natural narcotic,
Leave an unquenchable hunger for more.

MEMORY (HAWAII)

Palm trees bend, shake, rustle tunes that
Whisper like tiny whistles through fronds.
Your body like a floral island,
Where eager castaway fingers sink into sands
Inhaling exotic nights, exhaling rabid romance—
Eros entwined, shapes frolic, twist, turn.

Faceless days advance without numbers;
Tasks continue devoid of deadlines
Hawaii I long to pierce your lusty wilderness with
Temperate thoughts, plumeria leis commemorating ideals
Perfumed breezes accelerating as
They gust toward north shore.

May the fantastic return with clarity,
Latch onto winners, losers, dreamers
Provide fanciful fodder—enabling those
Who dwell in tropical mists,
Engulfed by naked forest ferns, time for
Jettisoned memories and lost opportunities.

V
URCHINS

Jigging It

        Grandma accumulated jigsaw puzzles,
        1,000 piece collector's editions
featuring landscapes, portraits, landmarks,
houses, that she and three aunts
        assembled just once
        then packed away forever,
        stored beneath the house
        like scenic cardboard time capsules of
        remembrance—afternoons, days,
        weeks, months. A reliable social engagement,
a group effort to fit the
right shapes together,
tip teacups
        toast sherry glasses
        share provocative gossip, start rumors,
show off family photographs,
especially grandchildren.

        The basement cabinet, like
        a giant safe deposit vault,
            reverently held each
            mint-condition box.
        Wilbur, his sisters, brothers, and I
        descended the icy cellar steps,
        snuck into the underground
            enchanted chamber that
            dared us, tempted us, encouraged us to
            enter. Facing no resistance, our
        tiny hands pillaged those puzzles—
            dumped contents on the
            cold, grey cement, pondered.

        Jigsaw possibilities
        selected from over 72,000 pieces.
   forced puzzle-parts together,
   bruised edges of subtle interlocking tiles,
   pushing and joining deformed male/female links, leaving
        spacious gaps and curled cardboard— our aggressive
        grouping evolved into an eclectic, textured mosaic of
        leaves clothing shoelaces sunsets gothic columns animals
   body parts old barns and automobiles, all colorful
    cutouts from master pictures scattered about the underground room
victorious adventurers, proud of our adult accomplishment,
we reshelved box after empty box like diligent little librarians,
   waded through the massive mixed
   mound of puzzle pieces,
   tossed them into the air like confetti, then
   dragged our exhausted bodies upstairs where
Grandma sat solving a new puzzle, knowing she'd still
love us—her *grandkids*—unconditionally.

EXCEPTIONAL SIGHTS

for Sei Shonagon

Not a day transpires without
  Encountering exceptional images:
Kittens nuzzling Elderly legs
  Lined with varicose highways;
Sail boats etching lines atop the
  Glass smooth seas, so silent, so still;
Coal miners warming sooty faces in
  Honeyed sunrays—a momentary reprieve from below;
Birds building traditional nests on concrete and steel
  Materials of unimaginative modern architecture
Majestic silhouette of Buddhist temples—Gothic Churches
  Against the bloodshot gaze of crimson skies
Spanish leather boots blazing away—a parking lot Paso Doble
  Double handholds alleyway *merengue*
Children fleeing from the icy surf
  Rolling in and out with a common tide.
Homeless people assisting accident victims in
  The freezing cold, without food in their stomachs.

BIG APPLE AD LIB

Comedy club managers book novice acts
No Jerry Seinfeld, Margaret Cho,
Richard Prior, Ellen DeGeneres—zero
Blue-collar comedians—
Just *Brady Bunch* brats making
Silent, unheralded comebacks, or
Letterman rejects,
Exploring another venue.

Witty humor strays on the
Just legal crowd, an
Inebriated audience jeers,
Heckles—creates sounds that
Pierce and deflate confidence in an instant
Make the room seem to shake like
Seismic waves at an
Earthquake's epicenter.

Till the headliner hops on stage
Surveys those seated and the toxic situation
Scraps prepared material
Isolates a longhaired man wearing
A Joe Cocker tie-dye t-shirt, then
Begins the Willie Nelson/hippie jokes
While the crowd appreciatively buys drinks for the
Butt end of the comic's humorous insults.

Backlash after ten minutes
Once refreshing, the "one joke"
Improv becomes stale [goes over like flat beer], and
Like time travelers,
Deep belly laughter and ear-to-ear smiles
Fade into the distant past
Return to the initial hostile mood—
Opening moments of the routine.

WHITE COFFIN

Cool white coffin
deep-freeze in the summer
becomes a weigh station of comfort
privileged by age;
we all feign eagerness as
opportunity surrenders us, individually,
to the massive, snowy tomb

We each take our turn
climbing into the abyss
every hot sweaty sibling
nestles with frozen string beans,
venison, pork, and day old bread—
like a giant tongue licking a metal ice tray—
stuck immobile, watching the lid lower,
hearing the lock snap,
listening to muffled sounds grow faint and disappear

Three times around the house the rest ran
dog, raccoon, and cat in tow
eternalizing coffin occupants,
unsupervised summer changelings, in
sixty-second blizzards—blizzards
even our pets experienced

In a ribbed cage, alone, we protest, and
stretch our arms inviolate
towards frost bearded steel windows,
imagining the sight of our own breath,
wishing the light, for a moment, would glow, and
anticipating the arrival of young liberators who'd offer
another living corpse into hell's kitchen, and
exchange anxiety, bravado, and stealth for
a textured *elephant skin* body,
victorious—bluish-purple

Haiku Sixte

Haiku #1

Dark clouds clapping hands
Greyhound chasing quacking ducks
Earthworms moving soil

Haiku #2

Rose petals dropping
Brooks splintering alleyways
Boot heels finger earth

Haiku #3

Slight disturbance here
Yellow garden's naked child
Frozen taps and pipes

Haiku #4

Tipping chalices
Early evening ebon skies
Cats curled by warm fires

Haiku #5

Eyes that feel each smile
Little bright red envelopes
Round bellies, closed hands.

Haiku #6

Watsonville harvest
Portabella mushroom feast
Under thin gold leaves

Haunting the Dead

A magnificent array of flowers
adorned the porch where wood shingles,
twisted, grotesque, swollen with age
strove to bite into load-bearing beams—
nails bending, rust replacing the
steel teeth once vigorous, sturdy.

From uneven edges, dirt through
flower boxes pushed, while
stringy vestiges of shriveled roots hung
like copper-colored Christmas tree tinsel
flocking the planter's base, its
warped mitered corners, incongruous joints,
gaped—off kilter like fallen, splintered mine shaft timbers.

Woodland's children religiously watered the flowers, chanted,
"The Bernardes been dead twenty years, don't cha' know?"
before crossing the wretched threshold through
unhinged doors and glazed-glass windows.
Inhaling intoxicating belligerence, the smell of dust
showered over all, left them empowered, as
they tagged walls, overturned furniture,
pillaged cupboards, dumped dresser drawer contents.
took tire irons to the China hutch, and
hanged enemy effigies in closets—tribute to the
home's ghostly legacy.

Bones of the Bernardes' dwelling place
bent like bamboo rod bows,
cracks inched across windows like spider webs—
increasing parabolic curvatures and geometric designs—
bludgeoned plaster fell from walls,
exposing a bad comb-over of
splintered lathe.

When demolishing property under
death's mysterious guise became passé,
they quit ritually baptizing the life-affirming flower box, and
left the house to die in peace.

Placing a leaky hose inside the planter, the
Woodland gang turned the tap and scattered,
abandoning their rib cage handiwork,
convinced lasting beauty could flourish amid a
house they'd brought to ruin.

A Novice Caught Defacing Pictures

Warts can be tricky
Pimples are not personal
Stitches thought passé
Whiskers almost provincial;
Steve, I never touched your photo
It must have been Scott, Kevin, or Coco.

The Cockpit

Rich Little's in the cockpit—
The pilot's voice vibrates over the airline P.A.
A mixture of Maurice Chevalier, Gephart Pardeau,
Yves Montand, and Pepe Le Pew
All forced through the same blown speaker
Warbling . . . ,
Muttering a monstrous routine
trying to give it new life,
Hoping to play to his captive audience, a full house at that.

But passengers do their "best" Shirley Temple imitations in reply
Puckering their mouths in circles ("Oh my goodness! Oh my goodness!")
Or raise their eyebrows like Groucho Marx, letting
jaws fall to their shoulders, perplexed, amused, or a bit bewildered.
The flight attendant programmed to set everyone straight
On the safety features of flying
Attempts to follow the muffled, muddled verbal instructions; she
Buckles her "demo seat belt"
    When she should have pointed out the emergency exits,
Raises both arms and shoots imaginary pistols at the restrooms in the rear
    When she should have emphasized the use of flotation devices,
        cushions countless butts had farted into without regard
        to their potential future function,
Receives a philharmonic applause (the pilot's ultimate desire in life)
    When she tosses that yellow oxygen mask—
Resembling the ones we're told are hidden above our head—
    At the cockpit door . . . .

Oh, Rich Little's in the cockpit
We left Oral Roberts stretched faithfully back on the runway
And we'll be hearing from John Wayne, no doubt, no doubt,
As we touch down in Dallas at *High Noon*.

COSMIC COMMANDS

for My Mentors

"Gort: Klaatu barada nikto"
    Oh? I really want to stay awhile, learn what
    Separates Homo sapiens and Humanoids;
    Explore pathos, do my Bette Davis schtick
    Walk in darkness to a window, feel the
    Sun's fingers caress my smooth alloy face.

"Gort: Klaatu barada nikto"
    Sure thing, still, could you
    Permit me a bit more treasured time?
    I wanna become Fritz Lang's *Metropolis*
    Free fall from the Empire State Building
    Smitten by a beauty, laughing at bi-planes.

"Gort: Klaatu barada nikto"
    Come on now, give me a break;
    A fully functional Darth Vader prosthetic,
    I'd like to fulfill my thespian ambition,
    Star in *Rocky Horror Show,*
    Die crucified on a RKO transmission tower.

"Gort: Klaatu barada nikto"
    All right, all right . . . let's make a deal
    Just get me some metal trim—a romantic, robotic
    Ladylove—who'll short circuit my memory board,
    Dent my ferrous frame, bring a twinkle to fixed eyes,
    Inspire me to initiate Klaatu's resurrection.

VI
Vignettes

NETS

From cyberspace screens
Trojan horses impersonate
spy ware, disguise
themselves as friendly free
software—geeks bearing gifts—
roll their way around firewalls
worm their way into mashups.

Artfully flaming while
observing netiquette
pixeled friends slip one another
DSL cookies then moan as if
their collective unconscious had
shared an ultimate orgasm—or
tossed communal dice & crapped out.

Tunneling ipod voices enlarge like quasars
black holes, dark matter, curvatures—
poor orphan stepchildren in a
dysfunctional gravitational family—
link unlikely bedfellows
performance masters, illegal downloaders,
Multi-User Dungeons & Dimensions.
Here's to multitasking,
fruits from online fields,
spread before us like an
Internet harvest, a
virtual banquet of essential
Aliases, consensual vice &
real time virtue.

STIGMATA

Hoodies conceal hair locks to die for, or
Curls like yellowed, breathless grass
      They might be nuns—
      Yes could be nuns;
Ankle length black dresses
Cloak cover girl figures—
      Bodies conjure images:
      Silicon Valley sylphs
Carmelite cheerleaders who Trumpet
progressive church politics as
      Sure winners—like tennis balls
      Kissing chalk lines—they hit the mark,
Leave cosmopolitan calling cards from
Youthful novitiates, life long Sisters, Christ's brides.

MAGNOLIA MASSACRE

Long tooth squirrels lacerate
Majestic magnolias,
Full flower blossoms that
Float vertically as
They fall like silent,
Unique snowflakes on
Barren, brown earth;
Creamy velvet skin
Loses elasticity, turns
Burnt sienna as disciplined
Ants carry their diced ivory cargo
Beneath dry rocks and
Beetles fertilize next year's buds as
They did before bees dusted pollen.

PREFERENCES

Keira favored men with salt 'n pepper hair
Two-day stubble beards, baritone voices
Abercrombie clothes, polo shirts with flair
Well-lined leather wallets, limitless choices.

She bathed in virgin Eucalyptus oils
Immersed herself slowly in rainbow water
Then stroked long legs, lubricated each pore
As sensual as Aphrodite's daughter.

Daylight telemarketer daylight in silk pajamas
Rising when the sun took its well earned respite
Dancing all night long at the Copacabana
Keira networked her way through darkness and light.

HOLIDAY

Sizzling silence—
   that's what we shared.
Two bodies apart
   in a room.
With peeling wallpaper
   and chipped paint.
A chandelier
   wouldn't have made any difference.

SMOKING

I'm a black motorcycle
a loud, boisterous, chopped hog
choking and coughing
filling the air with toxic spittle,
oppressed by lack of appreciation

TUNNELS

As senility tunnels its way through my brain
       like an awl, punching, pinching, depressing the past
craftsmanship becomes more game than art:
       memory seeking constant renewal.

VEINS

Lately I've taken to a study of hands
Fingernails, knuckles, palms, and cuticles
Encircled in veins
Royal blue and prominent, often
Spread out like tree roots
Just below the earth's surface.

Pirate

Flashing flintlock powder pan,
Sulfur cuts through ashes and smoke
Saltpeter residue sparks romance—
Thundering cannons, battle at sea—
Hey, give me a little pirate security
Swashbuckling color to fortify aging bones;

Pierce my ears with golden hoops
Hand me a cutlass, strike and parry blows—
Let minds reminisce the silver screen—Barrymore
Fairbanks, Rathbone, Garbo, Powers, Knightly,
Flynn; yet
Place my Tortuga in San Francisco,
Dock my ship beneath the Golden Gateway

2008

for Reginald Lockett

As one shadow passes into twilight
Under night's ebon mantle
Can accolades be more or less fitting
Than sharper thoughts,
Critical reflections,
Active, creative minds?

You knew the students, spoke for silent voices
Brought poets, writers, journalists, performers—
Magic words—and other worlds before them;
Nothing could have been better except
More time with us.

Always arriving, always departing;
A military man's son—Hunter's Point and Oakland,
Hawaii, Texas, and California—
Constant traveler, each base home, yet
As variable as ever changing seasons, from
A boy needing glasses to beret-wearing Black Panther,
Anne Heffley's mentee to Oakland's Poet Laureate.

Your words like trains, planes, and buses
Moved listeners to diverse destinations; you drew
Inspiration out of life's inequities
Where the blues cried out for examination
Realities, confrontations, resolutions—three different
Chords—played over a twelve bar scheme.
Your life *like jazz* created and progressed
Responding to a final corporeal note,
Possibly the beginning of another.

Sing wild and well as you exit the WordWind Chorus,
Poetry Readings, Classroom Creativity;
Places to match face and form,
Deep, booming voice and vignettes.
Leaving us one last over the shoulder laugh

Sterling Warner

Over the last 30 years, Sterling Warner has taught a wide variety of Composition, Literature, Creative Writing, and Rhetoric courses at two- and four-year colleges and universities. The author of fiction, non-fiction, and poetry, Warner's works include: *Thresholds* (© 1997), *Projections: Brief Readings on American Culture* (2nd edition © 2003), *World Literature and Introduction to Theatre* (5th edition © 2008) and *Visions Across the Americas* (8th edition © 2013). His poems have appeared in several literary magazines and journals, including *In the Grove, The Chaffey Review, Leaf by Leaf, The Monterey Poetry Review, inside english, The Messenger, Faculty Matters, The Atherton Review*, and *Metamorphoses*. Additionally, Warner also written three collections of poetry: *Without Wheels* (In the Grove Press © 2005), *ShadowCat: Poems* (Maple Press © 2008), and *Edges: Poems* (Maple Press © 2012)—as well as *Memento Mori: A Chapbook* (Maple Press © 2010). A Jim Herndon Award recipient (2013) as well as a Hayward Award winner (2000), Warner was named the Atherton Poet Laureate in 2014. Currently, Warner teaches in the English Department at Evergreen Valley College, where he has served as the Creative Writing Program Director, The Evergreen Valley College Author's Series Organizer, the *Leaf by Leaf* literary magazine the *Evergreen Valley College Annual Spring Poetry Festival* Coordinator.

www.ingramcontent.com/pod-product-compliance
Lightning Source LLC
Chambersburg PA
CBHW061339040426
42444CB00011B/3001